Welcome

Published under licence by Brown Dog Books and The Self-Publishing Partnership, 7 Green Park Station, Bath BA1 1JB

www.selfpublishingpartnership.co.uk

ISBN paperback book: 978-1-83952-280-2
ISBN e-book: 978-1-83952-282-6

Cover and internal design by Heidi Nowak

Printed and bound in the UK
This book is printed on FSC® certified paper

MIX
Paper from
responsible sources
FSC® C022913

LET'S ALL GROW A RUNNER BEAN

Frank's Book

LET'S ALL GROW A RUNNER BEAN

Grow with love

BROWN
DOG
BOOKS

Sometimes, encouraging too much growth can make picking your runner beans more of a challenge!

-Me *2021*

Why I Chose A Runner Bean

People have asked me, 'what on earth inspired you to write a book about growing a runner bean?' Runner beans have been a joyful ingredient for my family and a huge part of my upbringing.

Your runner bean can be grown from a city window box, a planter on the windowsill, a patio pot, an allotment or your garden. You may hear your bean shouting as it grows, 'Get rid of your winter blues! Smile! spring and summer are here!'

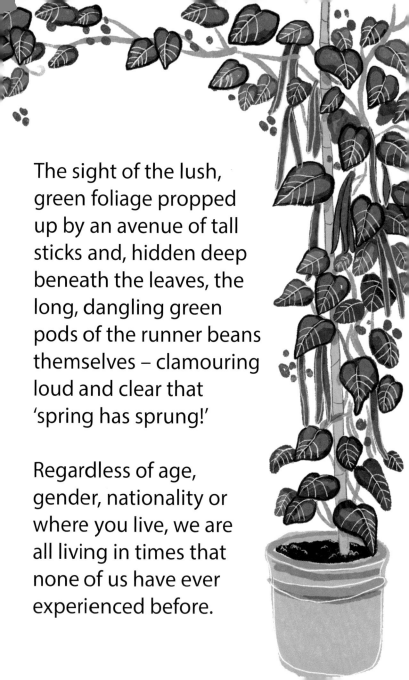

The sight of the lush, green foliage propped up by an avenue of tall sticks and, hidden deep beneath the leaves, the long, dangling green pods of the runner beans themselves – clamouring loud and clear that 'spring has sprung!'

Regardless of age, gender, nationality or where you live, we are all living in times that none of us have ever experienced before.

For some of us, the humble runner bean brings nostalgia flooding back – and for our children, it teaches an invaluable lesson about nature, growth and the fruits of your labour.

I quite simply wanted to bring some of that love, fun, happiness, hope, sharing, camaraderie and simplicity back into today's complicated lives.

I have always been a gardener, and find the pastime therapeutic and rewarding. Now, I wish to share this love with others. And what better way of bringing us all together, and sharing with our friends, family, neighbours and children, than by growing a runner bean plant from seed?

We can all enjoy the thrill of producing some homegrown food, bringing something in from the great outdoors, and helping Mother Nature to simply do what she does best.

By joining in on social media, we can all record our successes, challenge our family and friends, brag about our beans and share this simple pleasure with one another.

And that boys and girls, ladies and gentlemen is why I wrote:

'Let's All Grow a Runner Bean'

It matters not whether you are growing your runner bean in a city window box, on your windowsill, in an allotment or in your garden.

The therapeutic benefits of growing a plant for food are universal – it naturally creates relaxation, friendship, reward and passion, making it an experience totally unique to any other.

-Me 2021

From window box, patio pot,
to the garden.

How To Grow A Runner Bean

Seed Selection

As a family, we still plant an old variety of seed called *Scarlett Emperor*. It has a red flower which I think attracts the bees more!

The varieties of runner bean seeds are virtually endless; I find the easiest way to grow beans is to buy a couple of packs of different varieties, and share them with neighbours and friends. This way you can find the variety which suits your green fingers best!

If you are short of space, a dwarf variety is a good option.

Seed Pots & Containers

We always use wooden seed trays, which can be used from season to season, and for many other jobs around the garden.

With recycling in mind, the centres of old loo rolls and disposable cups both make exceptionally good containers. I just tell people to be imaginative ... make it fun!

If you intend to grow your runner beans in a tub or pot, they need to be a minimum of 23cm across and slightly deeper.

When and How to Plant

Be guided by the weather. Runner beans LOVE being watered, but cannot stand frost. We like to sow our seeds in mid-May to plant out in June. Planting out can continue until the end of July.

The soil temperature should be around 11–13 degrees centigrade for transplanting. They will take about 7 days to germinate, and about another 10 days before being ready to harden off. From early June I plant seeds directly into the garden.

12 °c

Fill your chosen seed container with soil or compost of your choice to approximately 8–10cm deep. Make a small hole about 5cm deep (I just use my finger), place the seed in the hole, and re-cover with soil/compost. Use one seed per pot, or 10cm spacing between seeds.

Now you have a good excuse to meet up with the other gardeners – we love sitting down chatting over a cuppa and a slice of cake, and putting the gardening world to rights!

Hardening Off

Hardening off is quite simply the way of getting the runner beans ready for the outdoor life! It is done by putting them outside through the day, and bringing them back in at night. Never leave them out when windy, or the stems may become damaged, and always bring them in at any sign of frost.

The whole process should take two to three weeks; eventually, you can leave them out full time.

A good chat, and the sharing of one's thoughts with others over a cuppa and a piece of cake, has solved many a problem!

-Me 2021

Relax

you deserve it!

Windowsill

We just leave our beans on the windowsill to germinate at a temperature of 12–15 degrees centigrade.

The trick with watering is little and often, keep the soil/compost damp but not flooded.

From emergence of the plant, turn the containers daily so the plant receives even light.

Transplanting from Pot to Garden

If grown in a windowsill container or small garden, or they are a dwarf variety, your beans can remain in their pots. All other beans will require a cane or stick to climb up. Before transplanting to the garden, your runner bean trench and canes/sticks will need to be in place.

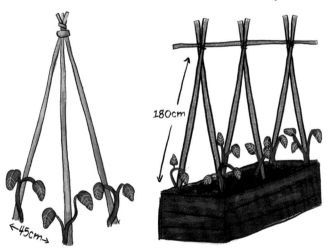

180cm

←45cm→

A deep bean trench
— plenty of well-rotted
compost and manure
is essential!

-Me 2021

COMPOST &
MANURE

Jack Frost

Do not be too KEEN – make sure all the frosts have gone before planting outside. I am ALWAYS too keen, and very often lose plants to Jack Frost! Old sayings, like 'Never shed a clout until May is out', are very relevant here.

To transplant, simply ease the plant from its container (be careful with the root structure), make a suitable size hole with a trowel about 5–8cm away from the cane/stick, place the plant in the hole, and firm the soil around the plant with your fingers.

←5–8cm→

When all the runner bean plants are in, water them well, but gently, with a fine-rose watering can.

As your Runner Bean Grows

You may have to guide you plant around the cane or stick to help it start to climb.

Water regularly – we do ours in the evening, and during extremely hot weather spray the flowers with a fine mist to help them set.

When the runner bean plant reaches the top of the cane or stick, pinch off the 'leader' at the end of the plant, as it will encourage more prolific lower growth, and hopefully more beans.

Pinch the leader

When to expect Runner Beans

The first small runner beans will appear around 6–8 weeks after sowing, and they'll be ready to pick at around 12–15 weeks.

A word of advice: pick regularly. Do not let beans get too old, or they will become tough and stringy.

Wishing you happy growing, picking and eating!

-Me 2021

A Very Special Gift

A gardening friend of mine once gave me a piece of lifelong advice, which I have passed on to many others:

'Always be honest to both yourself and those around you, NEVER EVER be AFRAID to ask for HELP and ADVICE.'

My friend finished the conversation by saying:

'Always remember that the knowledge, help and love given by a FRIEND is a VERY special GIFT – treasure it always.'

-Me 2021

My Runner Beans are Always Thirsty

Space for

your runner

bean memories

and notes.

-Me 2021

Never be afraid to share!

Like us, runner beans
appreciate a little love,
care and affection.
X X X
—Me 2021

Love, Care and Affection

Thankyou

for growing a

Runner Bean

-Me 2021

Written by

Frank Shellard (Me 2021)

Heidi Kim Illustrations